Comets
and Meteors
VISITORS FROM SPACE

An Earlybird Book
by Jeanne Bendick

Illustrated by Mike Roffe

THE MILLBROOK PRESS INC.

BROOKFIELD, CONNECTICUT

Cataloging-in-Publication Data

Bendick, Jeanne
Comets and meteors: visitors from space/by Jeanne Bendick
32p.; ill.: (Early Bird Books)
Includes index
Summary: Simple answers to children's questions about comets and
meteors. What are they? Where do they come from? Where do they
go? Why do they glow?
ISBN 1-56294-001-5
1. Comets. 2. Meteors. 3. Outer space. 4. Astronomy. I. Title. II. Title:
Visitors from space. III. Series.
1991
523.6 BEN

Published by The Millbrook Press Inc, 2 Old New Milford Road, Brookfield,
Connecticut 06804, USA

Produced by Eagle Books Limited, Vigilant House, 120 Wilton Road,
London SW1V 1JZ, England

Contents

Look! A Comet!

This is what a big, bright comet looks like in the sky.

Long ago, people thought a comet was a warning that something terrible was going to happen on Earth. It might be an earthquake, a flood, or maybe a war. Why else would a flaming ball suddenly appear in the sky?

Today we know much more about comets.
A comet is not a warning of bad things to come.
And we know that comets do not appear suddenly.
We just don't notice them against the stars until
they are near the Sun.

A scene from the 11th-century
Bayeux tapestry.

hAROLD

7

Where Do Comets Come From?

Astronomers are scientists who study the planets and stars. They think that comets are made of bits of rock, dust, ice, and gas that were left over when the **Solar System** formed about 4½ billion years ago. The Solar System is the Sun and its family of planets and moons.

Scientists think that far out in space, out past the farthest planet from our Sun, there is a huge cloud of comets wrapped around our Solar System. There may be billions of comets there, moving around like a giant swarm of bees.

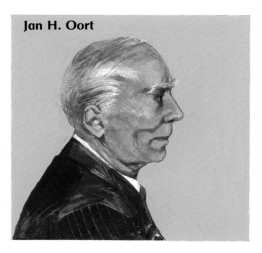

Jan H. Oort

The Oort cloud was named after a Dutch astronomer, Jan H. Oort.

The Oort cloud may be like a giant shell around the Solar System.

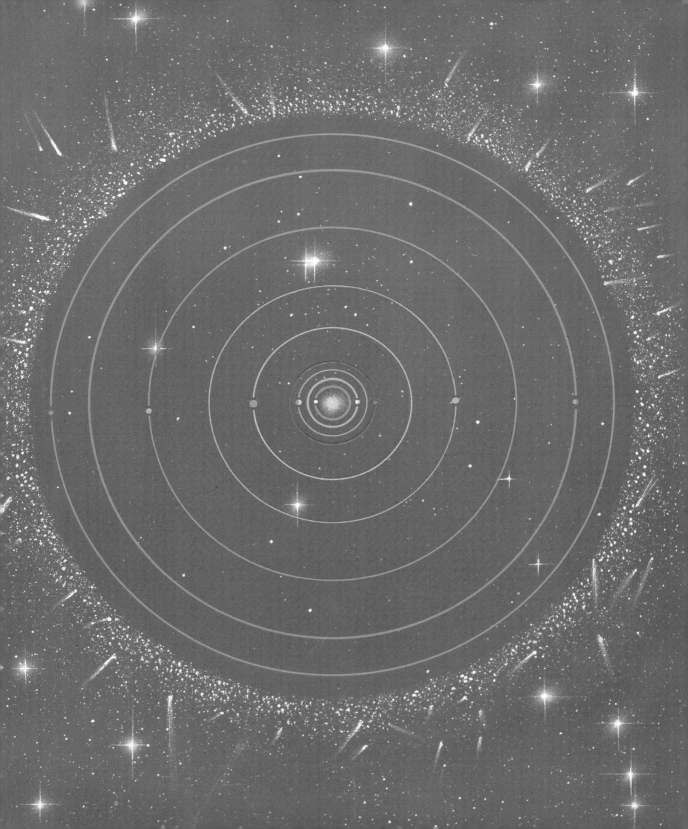

A Comet Starts Its Travels

Once in a while, some faraway star gives a sudden push or pull that can yank a comet out of the comet cloud. The comet may shoot off into space. Or it may start moving through the Solar System, toward the Sun.

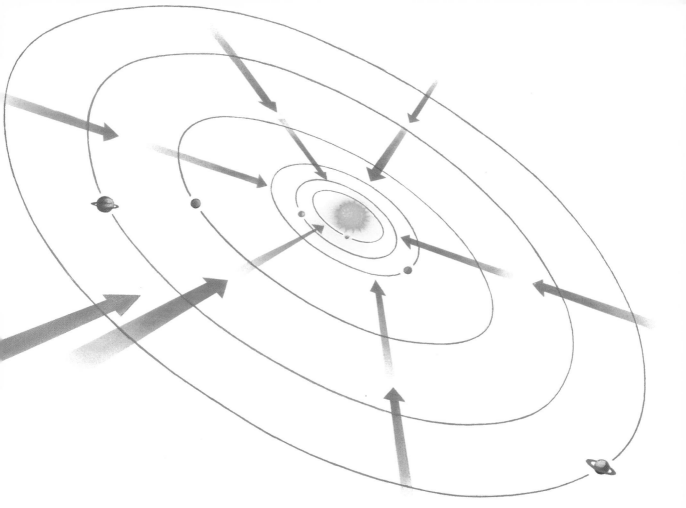

Everything in the Solar System is connected to the Sun by a force you cannot see. This force is called **gravity.**

The Sun's gravity pulls on the planets and their moons. It pulls on the flying rocks in the Solar System called the **asteroids.** It pulls on comets. It pulls them all toward the star that is the center of our Solar System. That star is our Sun.

Comets Change

gas tail

The gas tail is so thin, the stars show through it.

dust tail

Some comets look like fuzzy balls.

Some comets look like long-haired stars.

A comet starts out as a ball of frozen gases. One astronomer calls comets "dirty snowballs."

That dirty snowball is the **nucleus** of the comet. It is the seed around which the rest of the comet grows. It may be a big seed — a mile or even a few miles wide.

nucleus —

coma —

As the comet comes closer to the hot Sun, the ice begins to melt. The frozen gases spread into a misty cloud around the nucleus. That cloud is called the **coma.** The coma may be half a million miles across.

Part of the coma is pushed behind the comet. A force from the Sun called the **solar wind** blows this **tail** out behind the comet.

Most comets grow two tails or more. One tail is gas. It is straight and long — maybe 10 million miles long.

The other tails are shorter and curved. They are made of dust.

The tails of a comet always point away from the Sun. After the comet loops around the Sun, the solar wind blows the tail out in front of the comet.

What Makes a Comet Glow?

Out in space, comets are dark. They have no light of their own.

As they approach the Sun they begin to glow. The icy particles reflect the sunlight.

Comets reflect sunlight even at night. Reflected sunlight also makes our Moon and the planets shine. Only stars have their own light.

Something else makes comets glow. The gas in the coma soaks up some of the sunlight. It becomes like the gas in a fluorescent light bulb. It glows.

Earth

Moon

Venus

Sun

Mercury

17

About Orbits

The planets move around the Sun in regular paths, called **orbits.** The orbit of a planet is almost round. When a planet orbits the Sun once, it is a **year** on that planet.

Comets also move in orbits around the Sun. Their orbits are shaped more like eggs. These orbits are called **ellipses.** Comet orbits may be really long, if the comet starts far out in space.

Planets have almost circular orbits.

A comet's orbit is usually an ellipse.

Some comets take thousands or even millions of years to complete their orbits. Other comets take only a few years. Their orbits might crisscross the orbits of the planets. The time it takes a comet to complete its orbit is called the comet's **period.**

Comets move fast. But they seem to almost stand still in the sky for many nights in a row. They do not seem to move because they are so far away. Doesn't the Moon seem to stand still, too? You have to watch it for a long time to see that it is moving.

The Most Famous Comet

Certain comets appear in the sky again and again. We can predict when they will come. These comets are usually given names. Comets are usually named for the people who saw them first.

The most famous comet is called Halley's Comet. We see it about every 76 years, when it comes closest to the Sun. Its period is 76 years.

Halley's Comet passed us in 1985-86. It will come again in 2060. How old will you be then?

Edmund Halley

What Happens to Comets?

When comets come close to the Sun, the Sun boils away some of the gas in the coma and tail. Bits of dust and rock are blown away from the nucleus. This leaves a trail of comet matter along the comet's orbit. Those pieces, called **meteoroids,** keep on orbiting.

When the Earth passes through their orbit, the meteoroids glow. That's because the Earth is wrapped in a blanket of air called the **atmosphere.** When the meteoroids enter the atmosphere, air particles rub against them. The meteoroids get hotter and hotter until they start to burn. Then they are called **meteors.**

atmosphere

Beyond the atmosphere is space.

Some people call meteors "shooting stars" or "falling stars." They are not shooting or falling stars. Stars don't fall. You are seeing meteors.

Sometimes the Earth passes through the orbit of a melting comet. Then you might see **meteor showers.** Some meteor showers take place at the same time every year.

23

What Are Meteorites?

Can you think of anything that has different names at different times?

Water is like that. It is *water* when it is a liquid, *ice* when it is frozen, and *steam* when it is a gas.

water ice steam

in space,
meteoroids

in the atmosphere,
meteors

when they land,
meteorites

The chunks of matter out in space are a little like that, too. When they are in space, outside Earth's atmosphere, they are called *meteoroids.* When they are burning in the atmosphere, they are *meteors.*

Some meteors burn up completely. But others land on Earth. These are called **meteorites.**

The Asteroids

Meteor showers are from comets that have broken up. But meteoroids can come from any direction at any time. They may have nothing to do with comets. They may come from the **asteroids.**

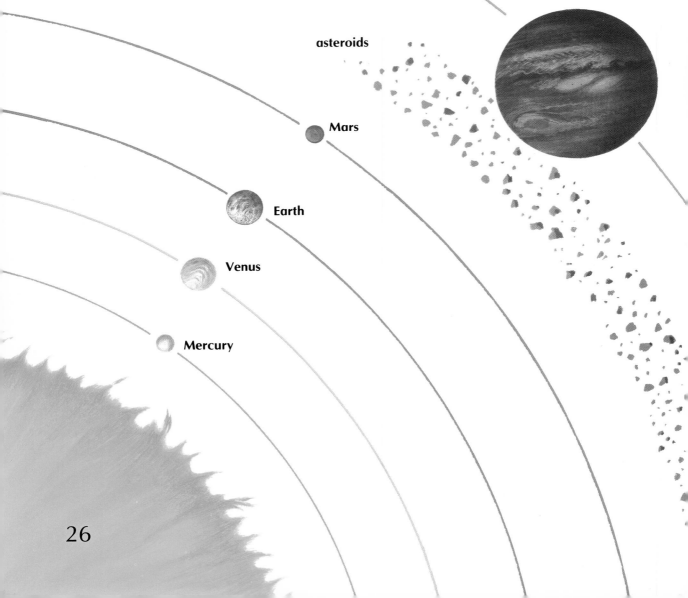

Jupiter

asteroids

Mars

Earth

Venus

Mercury

The asteroids are thousands of rocks that tumble around in their own orbits. These orbits are between the orbit of the planet Mars and the orbit of the giant planet Jupiter.

Most scientists think that the asteroids formed when the Solar System and comets formed. They are chunks of rock and metal that never came together to make a planet or a moon.

Sometimes asteroids bump into each other or fly off and crash into planets or moons. Our Moon has been hit so many times in the past that it is punched full of big holes, called **craters.** The Moon has no atmosphere to burn up rocky chunks before they come crashing down.

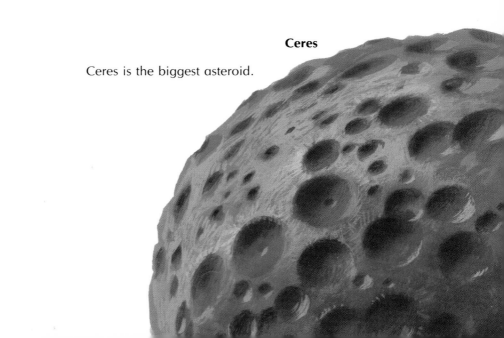

Ceres

Ceres is the biggest asteroid.

Meteorites on Earth

About 500 meteorites a day make it through Earth's atmosphere without completely burning up. Usually, they are very small — no bigger than snowflakes or grains of sand.

Most meteorites fall into the seas that cover so much of our planet.

Crater Lake

Once in a long, long while a really big meteorite falls on land. It might make a hole big enough to become a valley or the bottom of a lake. It may knock down a forest or raise enough dust to blot out the Sun for a while.

Lucky for Earth, it's a long time between big crashes — maybe a million years or more.

Some people think that the dinosaurs became extinct after a huge meteorite crashed into the Earth. Huge clouds of dust blotted out the Sun for a long time.

Will you ever find a meteorite? Maybe. Some look like stones and some look like chunks of iron. Some are made of both stone and iron. You can see different kinds of meteorites in museums.

The Hoba West meteorite in Namibia, Africa, is the largest known.

Will you ever see a comet? Maybe. But comets that are easy to see don't come very often.

In the meantime, you can see meteors. Some people think you can wish on them. Maybe you can wish to see a comet.

31

Index